S0-FAF-872

 **and God created...**

and God created...

written and illustrated
by
David Melton

Published by Independence Press, Drawer HH, Independence, Missouri 64055

Copyright © 1976
David Melton

All rights in this book are reserved. No part of the text or illustrations may be reproduced in any form without written permission of the publishers, except brief quotations used in connection with reviews in magazines or newspapers.

Library of Congress Cataloging in Publication Data

Melton, David.
   And God Created...

   1. Creation.   I. Title
BS651.M43   213   75-8945
ISBN 0-8309-0144-2

Published by Independence Press, Drawer HH, Independence, Missouri 64055
Printed in the United States of America
Designed by David Melton

Acknowledgments

Many people contributed to this
work. The author deeply appreciates
the efforts, the joyous attitudes,
and the influence these people so
generously gave:
Nancy Melton,
Mary Jane Fulton Prall,
Barbara and Ronald Noel,
Jim and Clare Tompkins,
Bud and Beverly Kimes,
Teresa Melton, Todd Melton,
Marguerite Melton, Denny Melton,
Ruby Thatch, Raymond Thatch,
and Mary Etta Pearson.

To Mary Jane

For years I have wanted to compose a book based upon the Genesis account of the creation. I wanted the pages to come alive with motion and color and the images to be both realistic and symbolic. I wanted the reader's imagination to be excited with the turning of each page. Most of all, I wanted the reader to be thrilled by the wonders of God's creation.

If, during the course of reading this book, you and members of your family become involved in discussions about God and how He affects our lives, then it is serving the purpose for which it is intended.

If you enjoy looking at this book one-tenth as much as I enjoyed developing it, then surely it will become one of your prized possessions.

—David Melton

the beginning

In the beginning,
God created the universe
and the world.

And the world
was without form
and it was surrounded
by darkness.

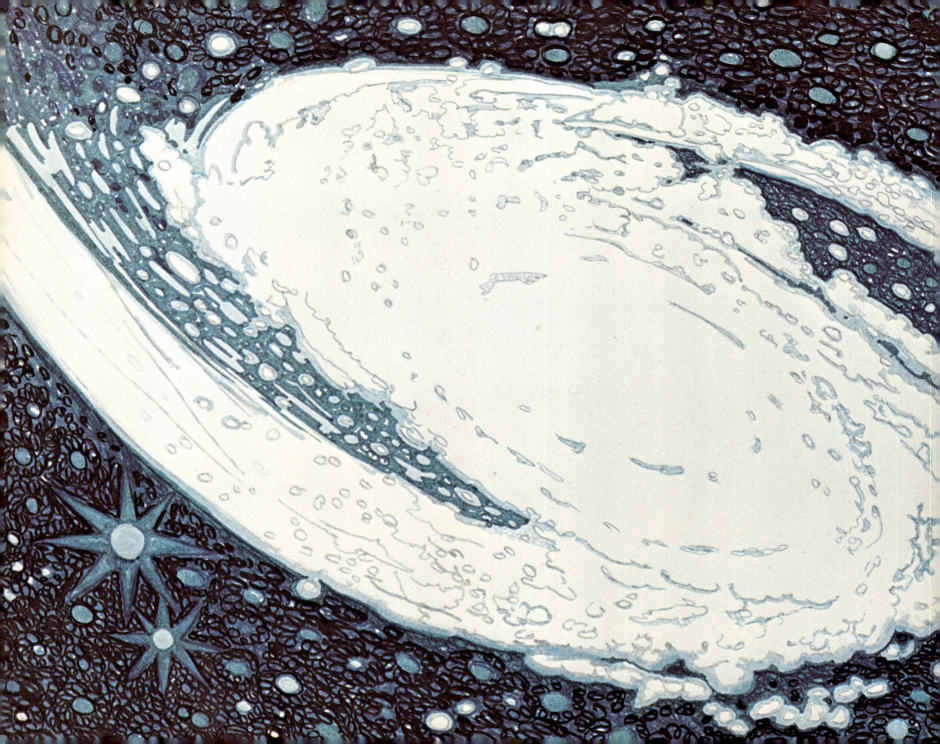

And God said,
"Let there be light."
And there was light.
When God looked at the light,
He saw that it was good.
So He divided
the light from the darkness.
He called the light day
and the darkness He called night.
And that time which was
between the first morning
and the first evening
He called the first day.

And the Spirit of God
moved throughout
the vastness of space.
And God said,
"Let there be stars and planets
to divide the distance."
Masses of energy burst forth,
forming stars and planets.
Fiery comets
streaked into orbit,
and there was great motion
throughout the universe.

God looked at His creations
and He was pleased.

Then God said,
"Let the waters
be divided from the lands
of the earth."
At His command,
mountains burst forth
from the storm-tossed seas,
and oceans were forced back
by the onrush of rocky shores.

And God saw
that it was good.

Then God said,
"Let the lands bring forth
grass and trees—
and the grass
will multiply
and grow,
and the trees
will bring forth fruit.
And the fruit
will bring forth seeds.
And the seeds will grow
to be like the plants
from which they came."

And it was done.

And God said,
"Let the lights
of the stars
and the suns
which move
through the universe
mark the passing of time.
And let them be the signs
for seasons,
and for days,
and for years."

And it was done.

19

Then God looked
at the waters
of the earth
and He commanded,
"Let the waters
bring forth
moving creatures
to live within
the boundaries of the seas."

And creatures were formed
and they moved
throughout the waters.

21

Then God looked
at the air which circled
above the lands
and the seas.
He commanded
that some creatures
should have wings
so they could fly
on the currents
of the winds.

And when He saw them
soaring through the air
with their wings gently curved,
He knew that it was good.

23

Then God looked
at the lands
of the earth
and He said,
"Let there be animals
of many kinds
to live upon
the hills and the plains.
Let the earth
bring forth
four-legged creatures
and crawling things.
And let each kind
multiply."

And it was done.

Then God said,
"From the earth,
I will make a man.
This man will
walk the lands
and he will
cross the rivers.
He will look
at all the other creatures
and he will see
what wonders they are.

"I will place
within this man
a spirit
which is like my own.
This man will be
a part of the world,
a part of the universe,
and a part of Me.

"This man
will be special
in many ways—
he will rule
the fish of the seas,
the birds of the air,
and the animals of the land.
All other creatures
will see his greatness."

So
from the elements
of the earth
God created a man.
And He breathed life
into the man's body
and He gave the man a spirit.
And God named the man—
Adam.

To provide a place
for the man to live,
God planted a garden
of great beauty
in the land
east of Eden.
In that garden,
every tree
and every flower
was pleasant to see.
And every fruit
was delicious to eat.

God said to Adam,

"Of every tree
you may eat the fruit,
except one.
In the center
of the garden
there is one tree
which you must not touch.
It is the tree
of both good and evil.
If you eat the fruit
from that tree,
your spirit
will be hurt,
and your body
will surely die."

Realizing that Adam
was only one of a kind,
God caused a deep sleep
to come over the man.
As Adam slept,
God took one of the ribs
from the man's body.
And with that rib,
God created a mate.
And he gave her to Adam.
When Adam saw her,
he realized
that she was made
from his own body—
that she was a part of him
and that he was a part of her.
And he called her <u>woman</u>.

And God said
to Adam and the woman,
"Look at the things
that I have given you—
every plant produces seeds
and every tree bears fruit.
All living things multiply.
So it will be
for you also."

In the garden
that God had given them,
the days of

Adam and his woman
were filled
with love and joy.

And so it was.
When the creation
of the universe
and the world
was finished,
and all living things
moved in peace,
God was pleased.
And He rested.

Of all the animals
on the earth,
the serpent
was the most deceptive.
One morning,
when the woman
was walking alone
in the garden,
the serpent
came to her
and asked,
"Did God tell you
that you could
eat the fruit
of all the trees
in the garden?"
The woman answered,
"We were told
we could eat the fruit
from all the trees
except the one
which stands
in the center
of the land.
If we eat
or even touch
the fruit of that tree,
we will surely die."

The serpent laughed
and then said,
"Do you really believe
that if you eat
the fruit of that tree
you will die?
You won't,
and God knows
you won't.
He also knows
that when you eat
that fruit,
you will be given
special knowledge
and you will
become as wise
as God Himself."
The woman wondered
if the serpent

spoke the truth.
She walked to the center
of the garden
and looked at the tree.
Its branches were heavy
with large round fruit
which was
pleasing to look at
and tempting to touch.
And suddenly
the woman wanted
to be as wise as God.
So she picked
one of the fruit
and she ate it.

Then she took one to Adam
and he too
ate the fruit.

After they had eaten,
Adam and the woman
looked about them
and began
to see things differently.
Their thoughts
were different too.
Now they were able
to see evil
and they thought
only of themselves.
And for the first time,
they felt shame.
They no longer
saw their own bodies
as being beautiful and good.
Now they realized
that they were naked.
So they tied
fig leaves together
and covered their bodies.

Later in the morning
when they heard
the voice of God,
Adam and the woman
hid from Him.
When God called out,
"Adam, where are you?"
Adam answered,
"We heard your voice,
but we were ashamed
because we were naked.
So we hid from you."
And God asked,
"Who told you
that you should be
ashamed of your nakedness?"
"The woman told me,"
Adam answered.
"She gave me
fruit from the tree
and I ate it."

God looked at the woman,
and asked,
"Why did you do that?"
And she answered,
"The serpent told me to!
It bewitched me."
Then God
turned to the serpent
and said,
"Because you have done this
you are the lowest
of all animals.
From this time forward
you shall move about
on your stomach,
and you shall see
only the dirt before you.
From this day on
your children
and the children of the woman
will be mortal enemies."

Then God said to the woman,
"Your sorrow and your shame
shall be great.
For now you will bring forth
your children in pain.
And you will feel sadness.
Your needs will be
the responsibility
of your husband.
And he shall tell you
what to do."

And then God said to Adam,
"Because you listened
to the woman
and ate the fruit
the earth is cursed.
Thorns and thistles
will grow on plants.
You will have to work
to find food and shelter
for your family.
Your years will be numbered,

and you shall know death.
And when you die,
your body will return
to the earth
from which it came."
Finally,
God told them,
"Now that you can see
both good and evil,
you will have to live
with both forces."

Then, God sent Adam
and the woman
out of the Garden of Eden
to face the harsh elements
of the world.
They felt hunger
and they learned fear.
They worked in the fields
and gathered food.
They built a shelter
to protect them
from the cold nights
and from hungry animals.

45

However,
because God is
both loving and forgiving,
the days of Adam and Eve
were not entirely without joy.
As God had promised,
they had children.
And the children grew
and in turn
they had children.
And the descendants
of Adam and Eve
multiplied greatly in number.

And so,
according to the
book of Genesis,
began the family of Man.

About the Author

David Melton's range of creative expression seems to be without confining borders and limiting labels. He has the rare distinction of being recognized as an author, a poet, and an illustrator. One has only to review his list of credits to realize that he is one of the most prolific and versatile talents in today's literary scene.

To many, Mr. Melton is considered as an analyst and a commentator. In his books, TODD, WHEN CHILDREN NEED HELP, and CHILDREN OF DREAMS, CHILDREN OF HOPE, he surveys the problems facing parents of mongoloid and other brain-injured children in obtaining educational and medical treatment. In BURN THE SCHOOLS—SAVE THE CHILDREN, he explores the problems confronting the school systems, and the negative materials and attitudes which saturate those systems and limit children's rights to a joyous time of learning.

Mr. Melton's books of poetry, I'LL SHOW YOU THE MORNING SUN and JUDY—A REMEMBRANCE, quickly became best sellers, and his first juvenile book, THIS MAN—JESUS, is widely acclaimed for its sensitive retelling of the story of Christ, and for the boldness of illustrations which depict a strong, masculine Jesus.

Many of Mr. Melton's major illustrations have been reproduced for calendars, record covers, puzzles, note cards, national magazines, and book jackets.

Mr. Melton, his wife Nancy, and their two children, Todd and Teresa, live in the Midwest.